There Is No God
Or Is There?

Michael W. Newman

©2012 Michael W. Newman

Ursa publishing

Printed in the United States of America

ALL RIGHTS RESERVED.

No part of this publication may be reproduced, stored in a retrieval system, or transmitted, in any form or by any means—electronic, mechanical, photocopying, recording, or otherwise—without prior written permission.

For information:

www.mnewman.org

To George Hides and Benjamin Newman, grandfathers who helped weave the fabric of my life.

On the cover:
Benjamin Newman standing in front of his World War I truck
circa 1919

Contents

Preface	**7**
Chapter One: **Insanity**	**9**
Chapter Two: **Risk**	**19**
Chapter Three: **Rebuilding**	**29**
Chapter Four: **Destruction**	**39**
Chapter Five: **Change**	**49**
Chapter Six: **A Miracle**	**59**
Chapter Seven: **Proof**	**69**
Chapter Eight: **Assault**	**79**
Chapter Nine: **Endings**	**89**
Chapter Ten: **Testing**	**99**
About the Author	**109**

Preface

There is no god. Or is there?

Have you made that statement or asked that question? Have doubts filled your mind and soul? Have the pain and chaos of the world or the deep and abiding hurt in your heart convinced you that god does not exist?

Or has it been a simple conclusion based on scientific knowledge and observation? There is no one "out there." Facts are facts. The natural world is a remarkable place, but there is no need to attribute its wonder to a supernatural being.

Perhaps some motivation for distancing yourself from god is the damage done by religion over the centuries. Who needs a humanly constructed institution to wreak more havoc in the world?

Maybe you're indifferent about the god issue. Life is too important to get caught up in spiritual speculation and in narrow claims of truth and moral absolutes. It's much more crucial to make a difference in the world by living well and impacting others in a positive way.

If you find yourself in any of these intellectual or spiritual places, you may benefit from a short journey with my grandfathers. That's where this book will take you. It's a journey of love and loss, of murder and miracle. It's a journey that may cause you to think about life like you've never thought about it before.

Michael W. Newman

Chapter One
Insanity

Ω

Welcome to the nuthouse. That's how my mom referred to the general craziness and disorder that could be churned up by our family. My mother was one of ten brothers and sisters. She was number eight, the first of a second wave of children born to George P. Hides. The first seven children were from his first wife. The final three were from wife number two, my grandmother. I was one of thirty-nine grandchildren from this maelstrom of a large Greek family. Nearly one hundred of us would cram into a small row house on the west side of Chicago to celebrate whatever occasion happened to be upon us. Honestly, I don't know how all of us fit. And with all the Hides daughters, daughters-in-law, and additional very dramatic female family and extended family participants, I don't know how one bathroom sufficed.

The crowd could be intimidating. One Christmas, I decided to bring my baseball card collection to the annual Christmas dinner and hullabaloo. I don't know why I thought I would need a diversion or entertainment in the tumult of our traditional Christmas gathering, but my temporary insanity prevailed and I broke out my precious cargo in the corner of my grandparents' crowded living room. One of my cousins immediately pounced. With a fiendish grin, he picked up my box of baseball cards, turned it over, and laughed while he scattered Mickey Mantle, Ernie Banks, Denny McLain, and too many other players to mention all over the living room floor. I never really liked that cousin. But there were plenty of others to choose from. In fact, in spite of the occasional intimidation from the big kids, I liked this family. There was never a dull moment. Laughter, conversation, dancing, great food, and unceasing motion were staples of every gathering. This was a family with life, zest, and fervor. Utter madness prevailed. And it was kind of fun.

I credit my grandfather for setting the tone. George Hides was a man of action. He was always on the move. With his signature cigar tucked into one corner of his mouth, he bounced from person to person, grandchild to grandchild. His gruff voice and thick Greek accent echoed through the house. He never stopped.

An irrepressible entrepreneur, George started a grocery store operation when he was a young man. He moved on to running a produce route in Chicago, went back to the grocery business, and finally settled on the dry cleaning trade sometime in the late 1930's. Supreme Cleaners was located at 429 North Laramie Avenue. George ran the show while his wife Bertha, my grandmother, functioned as the seamstress.

I'll never forget the dry cleaning store. Racks of plastic-covered clothes filled the back room behind the counter. Each bundle of freshly cleaned and pressed garments had a number stapled to it, ready for customer pick-up. My grandfather could press a button and the clothes came to life, snaking their way along an electrically powered track until he matched the

Chapter One

customer's number with the bundle of cleaning. The lobby of the store was empty, except for a plastic chair or two for friends to sit in as they visited with my grandpa. His friend Nick loved to fritter away the day in conversation with George. Next to the cash register, framed and hung on the wall, was the first dollar bill earned from the cleaning business.

The store was old and beautiful. It had a high, ornate ceiling that was painted bright white. The exterior was typical "main street" brickwork, framing a large window with a bright neon sign. Supreme Cleaners was my grandfather's pride and joy.

But the action didn't stop there. The two-flat Chicago row house where we gathered for visits and celebrations was just about one block away from the store. This little enclave was the epicenter of my grandfather's bustling world. His oldest son, also named George, started a restaurant down the street from the dry cleaning store. It was aptly named "George's Grill." My grandfather's dry cleaners may not have provided me with loads of entertainment, but eating a cheeseburger and drinking a Green River soda at my Uncle George's grill was always a delightful treat. Uncle George lived in the flat above my grandparents. Another daughter and son-in-law lived down the street from them. The buzz of family business, conversation, arguments, work, and activity was always close by.

If all of that didn't fill the day for my grandfather, he made sure he had plenty of activity in his back yard. The narrow patch of land became his personal garden and vineyard. His house on Leamington Avenue had a small front yard and a brick front porch that was deadly when you tumbled off of it. I had the wind knocked out of me many times after flying backwards off of that porch. The narrow walkway between his house and the neighbor's led to an area that gave evidence of my grandfather's nurturing spirit. He had tomato plants that he cared for and treasured. But most fascinating to me was the fact that he grew grapes. Grapes in Chicago! Where the backyard led to the alley behind the house, my grandfather built a grape arbor. Whenever I exited the yard to play in the alley, I stared at the thick tangle of grapevines above me and around me. This little Eden in the middle of the concrete jungle of the city displayed the imprint of a man who not only never stopped moving, but who could be patient and caring.

Of course, he kept those qualities fairly well hidden. He was a visionary man who did not like to veer from his concept of what life should be like. He insisted on eating lamb every Sunday--even when the rest of the family had to make due with less expensive and less filling fare. He believed that women did not need education, so the Hides women took the home economics track at the high school and graduated to either marriage or to work in one of the family businesses.

His stubborn streak kept him in the city. My grandfather's business was in the Austin District of Chicago. This area of the city had been declining for years. The decade from 1960 to 1970 saw young families moving to lower-priced housing in the suburbs and gravitating toward the suburban

Chapter One

school system. Racial unrest also pushed many residents to the north, south, and west. I remember taking the train from our small home in the more affordable suburbs to visit my grandparents' home in the city. My father drove our family car to work, so my mother readied her three sons and led us on foot to the train station not far from our house. We boarded the train for the journey downtown. The green-tinted windows on the Chicago-Northwestern train cars made the view outside even more intriguing as the train glided smoothly toward our destination. The conductor clicked his ticket puncher quickly and efficiently as he made sure everyone had paid the proper fare. In his official blue hat and uniform, he called out stops along the way.

As the years went by, the decline was noticeable. Businesses were closing. Protective iron bars were appearing on windows of stores and homes. The corner vacant lot down the street from my grandparents' home was once a place where we could play until dark. It was now off limits. I remember the shocking news that my cousin Bobby was beaten severely by a gang of young men. Bobby was hospitalized and nearly lost his life. He was the son of my Uncle George and Aunt Mary. Not long after the violent attack on their son, they moved out of the neighborhood.

On many Sunday afternoons, my mother and father would load my brothers and me into the car for a trip to grandma and grandpa's. It seemed like such a long trek into the city. We passed railroad yards. We made our way around the electric CTA buses with their antennae-like wires sparking

There Is No God, Or Is There?

against the overhead electric lines that supplied their power. We drove past factories, through clusters of businesses on busy city streets, and by some beautiful parks. Outside one park there always stood a man selling colorful balloons. My mother told me that at one time one of my uncles had been the "balloon man." I knew things were changing when the balloon man disappeared. The crowds in the parks weren't as plentiful. I overheard my parents talking about how some of their favorite spots as children were now falling into disrepair and closing. Life was changing on the West Side of Chicago, but my grandfather gave no indication that he would give in to the pressure. His business would keep going. He was staying put.

After all, this was his neighborhood. Other businesses on Laramie Avenue were closing their doors, but not Supreme Cleaners. He had worked for decades to carve out his niche in Chicago. He had come a long way from herding sheep for his father in Greece. He was a businessman who was responsible for his community. For their sake, for the sake of the neighborhood, for the sake of his family, his establishment would stay its course.

But on Wednesday, April 22, 1970 everything changed. As the lunch hour approached, my grandfather's friend, Nick, chatted with him at the dry cleaners and my grandmother sat in the Corner Grill with my Uncle George and Aunt Mary. Just after noon, a young man stepped into my grandfather's dry cleaning store. The man's two friends waited outside. My grandfather looked at the young man and saw a gun in his hand. With the gun pointed at my grandfather, the brash robber

Chapter One

demanded all the money from the cash register. My proud, stubborn, tough, Greek grandfather paused. Would he cave in to this young intruder? Would he let this punk intimidate him? Would he surrender his hard-earned money? Would he compromise all he stood for to one cowardly thug who happened to darken the door of his business?

My grandfather thought, stared intently at the threatening stranger, and reached his hand toward a knife he had hidden under the counter.

Chapter One Discussion Questions:
Insanity

1. "Normal" life is filled with highs and lows, good times as well as adversity. Discuss how "normal" life can be disappointing as well as thrilling.

2. How might we mischaracterize "normal" life, leading us to disappointment and disillusionment?

3. Discuss one good development and one disappointment happening in your life these days.

4. George Hides forged ahead in the face of a declining neighborhood. What character qualities might have caused him to stick with his work?

5. George had a shadow side to his personality. How do you balance the positive and negative characteristics of your personality?

6. In your opinion, why do bad things happen?

Chapter Two
Risk

Ω

Taking risks was in my grandfather's blood. At the tender age of thirteen, he and his nineteen-year-old brother Steve boarded a boat in Patras, Greece to embark on a journey to the promised land: America. Since his birth on May 6, 1894 George lived in the small village of Neohorion. It was a one-sheep town that promised no wealth or future to the young men of the region. Word of treasure and opportunity had reached this little town tucked in the mountains of the Peloponnesus, the southern island home of the powerful Spartans of Greek history. George and Steve joined thousands of young Greek men on a quest to America in the early 1900's. They hoped to strike it rich and bring the bounty home for their struggling families.

After landing in New York, George's last name was promptly changed from the Greek Haidoutis to the Americanized Hides. New York was just a stopover for the Hides brothers, however. They quickly boarded a train and took it to the end of the line: Chicago. Chicago was where Greeks were gathering and succeeding. Since the Chicago fire in 1871, Greek men found jobs in construction as the city was rebuilt. Soon the Greeks began to dominate the produce market. From there, Greeks opened restaurants and other small businesses as they took the city by storm. George and Steve arrived in Chicago and jumped into the fray of independent businessmen. They got connected with the street vendor network in Chicago and began hawking their wares: fruit, vegetables, and any other food they could offer to make a profit.

Although work dominated their lives, George and Steve plunged into the new and exciting city life Chicago had to offer. Instead of connecting with the network of Greek community organizations and church groups, the teens struck out on their own. They valued the Greek community and traditions, but the excitement of the new world was too enticing for them to stay ensconced in a Greek cocoon.

It didn't take long for both brothers to meet girls. Steve met Helen Peterson, a young Scandinavian with an independent streak that wouldn't be tamed. Steve and Helen married in 1921 but divorced in 1928. Steve would spend the rest of his days as a single man.

George met a French beauty named Lila Rush. Perhaps their eyes met or hands touched when she and her family stopped to buy produce from George and his brother. Whatever happened in that first meeting, it didn't take long for sparks to fly. George found out where she lived and began to call on her as soon as he could. Her parents, Joseph and Marie, provided some stability for George. He became fast friends with Lila's three brothers and sister. But a stable family wasn't the key draw for George. Lila's sweet and simple beauty and her caring and gentle spirit overwhelmed George's heart. He fell head-over-heels in love.

Chapter Two

It didn't take long for George to ask for Lila's hand in marriage. He promised Mr. Rush that he would take good care of his daughter. Lila's father could see that she was smitten. So, in May of 1914, eighteen-year-old Lila Rush married twenty-year-old George Hides in a no-frills wedding ceremony at the Chicago City Hall. Marie Rush's pastor, a Lutheran minister, was asked to do the honors and agreed.

George was rooted. He was in Chicago to stay. While about one-third of his fellow Greeks returned to the homeland, George was one of the majority who found treasure in the United States. He had mastered the English language. He scrimped, saved, and scrapped his way to a successful start in business, and now he was with the love of his life. Looking into each other's eyes, George and Lila were committed to the next steps of the adventure together.

Suddenly, reality hit. Permits for selling food from street stands were being revoked. Italian food vendors, who once dominated Chicago's grocery distribution network, influenced the city's corrupt political system in an effort to put the Greeks out of business. This move sent George into quick decision mode. Time and money were running out. With some fast talk from him and a heavy dose of charm from Lila, they were able to rent a storefront and open their own grocery store.

By leaving Greece, George avoided being drafted by the Turkish army. The Turkish-occupied areas of Greece were attempting to conscript as many young Greek men as possible. Now, with not yet finalized status as a United States citizen,

There is No God, Or Is There?

George was not called upon by the United States for military service either. Instead of being summoned to serve in the burgeoning World War I effort, George and Lila pressed forward as partners in the new family business. And "family" became the operative word very soon. Just ten months after their wedding, Lila became pregnant.

The delight, adventure, and romance continued as George and Lila welcomed a baby boy on December 15, 1916. Their new son was a special Christmas gift. They named him George Steven Hides, the first of a new generation born on American soil. The new parents doted on their firstborn and had him helping at the grocery store as soon as he could walk. Little George had his mother's gentle features and deep brown eyes. The future looked bright as the Hides clan gained traction and dove into the thick of life as an American family.

George and Lila's love and partnership grew as each year passed. They cherished their time together. They enjoyed visits with Lila's family. And they loved to see their family grow. Another son, James, was born in January of 1919. Their first daughter, Dorothy, was welcomed two years later in January of 1921. A third son, John, came along in 1924. Two girls were added to the mix: Audrey in February of 1927 and Betty in November of 1928. But then, everything crashed.

The Great Depression hit hard. George's grocery store business slowed to a trickle of customers who were trying to get the most out of every penny. More and more friends and neighbors found themselves unemployed. Lila's brother Harold became so desperate that he changed his name back to its

Chapter Two

original form, La Roche, and ventured off to New York City to pursue fame and fortune. He was able to find work as a stage manager in the newly developing Radio City Music Hall.

But many others were not as fortunate. Unemployment in Chicago grew to fifty percent. With a total disruption of regular customers, George and Lila had to give up the grocery store. They couldn't afford the rent and had to do something drastic to stay afloat. George was thirty-five years old and Lila was thirty-three. They had six young children to care for. Times were desperate.

George decided to go back to his roots. When he first arrived in Chicago, he fended for himself on the streets. Now he would hit the streets again. He recruited his oldest son, now approaching twelve years of age, and together they began a hard-driving produce route. The customers may not have been able to come to him, but he could go to the customers. And go he did. Day and night George and his son worked to put food on the table. He did not come to the United States to fail. He came to earn a better life.

Secure in their new and even more frugal existence, Lila and George welcomed their seventh child in October of 1931. They named her Frances and delighted in her happy disposition. But something was wrong. Lila had trouble bouncing back from the pregnancy and birth. She seemed weaker during the months before Frances was born, but kept plugging away as a busy mother and active business partner. But after their seventh child came into the world, Lila was not the same. She experienced pain in her joints and shortness of breath. Her new

There is No God, Or Is There?

weakness left her confined to bed as she struggled with the pain. Soon, fever plagued her and the pain became more severe. Doctors did their best to make her comfortable, but Lila became weaker and frail. George couldn't believe this was happening. The love of his life seemed to be slipping away.

George worked harder than ever to keep the family afloat. Because he had to be on the streets to make sales, he asked a local teenager, Bertha Hoenig, to live with them and help care for the children. Bertha was eighteen years old. Her mother had just died, so she lived part of the time with an aunt and uncle and part of the time with her father. Bertha's life was up in the air. She craved some love and stability, so when George approached her about helping his family, she gladly agreed to lend a hand. She moved in with the Hides family and gave her all to care for the seven children ranging from an infant to a teenager, along with a very weak mother.

Just as the economy continued to deteriorate, Lila's health became worse as each week passed. George did his best to sit up with his wife during each night, holding her hand and stroking her feverish brow. Then, each morning, he grabbed a fresh cigar and pursued produce sales with his oldest sons. Weary and heartbroken, George kept pushing forward. His wife had to be getting better. She was only thirty-six years old. She had to rally. How would he ever go on without her?

On Sunday, August 28th, George stayed home with his family. Lila was worse than ever, but George tried to keep life as normal as possible for the children. After Sunday dinner, the lazy afternoon soon became evening and all the children went

Chapter Two

to bed. George took a seat next to the bed where Lila labored to breathe and intermittently moaned with pain. He took her hand and looked at her pale, thin face, still beautiful and delicate. They had been married for eighteen years--exciting, active, adventurous years, filled with risk and romance. Eighteen years--much too brief a time together. It couldn't be near the end, could it? In fatigue and worry, George dozed off, still clutching dear LIla's hand.

At two in the morning he awoke with a start. He looked at Lila. She was still, completely still. Her face looked peaceful, more peaceful than it had looked in months. Suddenly George realized that Lila wasn't breathing. He leaped out of his chair and ran to call the doctor. When the doctor arrived, there was nothing he could do. Lila's heart couldn't take the strain anymore. She was gone.

For the first time in a long time, George wept. He felt completely empty and lost without his dear Lila.

Chapter Two Discussion Questions:
Risk

1. Some would say that George Hides was a self-made man. What is your opinion?

2. Coming to America presented one challenge after another. How do you think the challenges shaped George's life?

3. How do challenges affect you--both positively and negatively?

4. On a 1 to 5 scale, with 1 being risk averse and 5 being a high risk taker, rate how risky you tend to be.

5. Discuss how you would adjust your tendency for or against risk.

6. Everything seemed to come crashing down for George. How does a person get through such devastation?

George and Lila Hides

Chapter Three
Rebuilding

Ω

How can anyone describe the feeling of losing your very heart and soul? My grandfather was in a daze. For the first time in his life he didn't know what to do. It wasn't supposed to be this way. He and his beautiful wife were just beginning their adventure. They wanted to grow old together. They wanted to see their children grow up, get married, and give them loads of grandchildren. George's heart ached. It was as if his soul collapsed inside. He felt like he could barely breathe. This sadness was something he had never experienced. A piece of himself was missing. Everything that kept him alive seemed to be hemorrhaging from every pore. George was devastated that he would never see his dear, sweet Lila again.

In the afternoon on Thursday, September 1, 1932, Lila's casket was lowered into the soft late-summer ground at Ridgewood Cemetery just outside the Chicago city limits. She was buried next to her mother as tears streamed down the faces of her emotionally battered family. Reverend Hunt, the pastor who married George and Lila at city hall, now stood over the grave and spoke some final words. Lila's seventy-nine-year-old father tried to keep his composure as he bade farewell to his little girl. Baby Frances had no idea what was happening. Betty was only three. Neither of the girls would remember their mother. The other children felt the pain deeply. There would be more pain to come.

There is No God, Or Is There?

George and the children went back home, but it didn't take my grandfather long to realize that he couldn't stay there anymore. Lila was everywhere. Her presence, her voice, her laughter, her handiwork, and even her pain filled each room. He couldn't take it. He had to get out. He also needed help. Even with Bertha's extra hands, the needs of seven children and the demands of providing for them were too much for him. George could barely get out of bed in the morning. How could he do the job of both mother and father? Six months after Lila's death, George sold his house and moved close to where his cousin John had a store. With the help of John and his wife, perhaps he could manage this new, turbulent, and dreadful life he had to live.

But he couldn't. He couldn't do it. The entrepreneur, the man of big risks and daring action, the immigrant who would let nothing defeat him, the father in the prime of his life was immobilized by loss that shattered his will to go on. The family was falling apart. One year after they moved--just eighteen months after Lila's death, George gave up. Lila's sister, Frances, traveled from New York to pick up her namesake, baby Frances Hides. Little Frances was taken to New York. George, my grandfather's oldest son, his partner in business, and his pride and joy was sent to a Civilian Conservation Corps camp in Galva, Illinois. The camp was for eighteen to twenty-five-year-old children of the unemployed. George was not yet eighteen when he was sent there, so he had to lie about his birthday. He would earn thirty dollars each month, twenty-five of that being sent back home to help fund the broken family. James and Dorothy, now fifteen and thirteen, stayed with their father.

Chapter Three

They were old enough to help the family get back on its feet financially. John, Audrey and Betty were brought to St. Paul Lutheran Church to be baptized at a hastily arranged afternoon baptismal service. Betty was then taken home by cousin John and his wife. Son John and daughter Audrey's fate brought more heartbreak to their father. They were taken to the Evangelical Lutheran Orphan Home in Addison, Illinois.

George swore that this would be a temporary arrangement, but he had no idea how he would ever bring his family back together. He could barely keep himself composed and functioning. Bertha went back to live with her aunt. My grandfather started to do what he did best: he worked.

Seeing his cousin starting to do well in the grocery business, George quit his street vendor work and transitioned back into owning a grocery store. Work was therapy for my grandfather. He poured himself into his business. He didn't want to be defeated. He desperately wanted his family to be back together. Perhaps if he worked hard enough, he could make everything right again.

Twice each month, on the second and fourth Sundays, George was allowed to visit John and Audrey. He and Bertha traveled to the Addison orphanage to spend four precious hours with the children. At five in the afternoon they had to say their good-byes for two more weeks. The visits tortured George. His own children were living as orphans. This couldn't go on. For their sake, for Lila's sake, he had to get them back. He had to bring the family back together.

There is No God, Or Is There?

George noticed how Bertha loved his children. She was caring and gentle. The children gravitated to her light-hearted personality and motherly spirit. While he was all business, she brought laughter and joy to them. She even began to help George feel some happiness. Maybe it was time. For the first time in over two years George saw a glimmer of hope. What if he and Bertha brought the family back together?

George ran the idea by Bertha. What if they were to get married? She was twenty-one years his junior. His oldest son was nearly as old as she was. Could this work? She loved the children. She hated to see the family separated. She witnessed George's care and compassion. He was a good man. Why not take this chance together? Why not begin an adventure with this man who lived for risks and new possibilities? Bertha said yes.

On May 24, 1935, George Hides and Bertha Hoenig were married. It was time for a new beginning. It was time to get the family back together. But this was easier said than done.

Five of the seven children were brought back home fairly quickly. But the two youngest, Betty and baby Frances, had become part of new families. George and Bertha wrote letters, visited, talked, and worked to convince each family that this arrangement was temporary. It was time to reunite all the brothers and sisters. After eight months, Lila's sister, in tears, brought Frances back home. Betty also finally made the transition from cousin John's home. By January 28, 1936, the family was together again. The family also began to grow.

Chapter Three

Five days after Betty walked through the doorway of the house on Parkside Avenue, Bertha, my grandmother, gave birth to Jeanne Marie Hides, her first daughter, my grandfather's eighth child, and my mother.

What a ride. My grandfather had gone from the loss of his first love and the surrender of his family to experiencing new love and starting a new family. For three and a half years, he had endured the extremes of raw emotion. He weathered some of the deepest lows imaginable, lows that cast him into hopelessness, confusion, and despair. In what seemed to be an endless journey of loss, he suddenly encountered new life, new love, and a new beginning. But my grandfather wasn't the type to pause and reflect on what had happened. If his emotions were tattered and worn, he didn't show it. He just kept pushing forward. He loved little Jeanne and delighted in a new baby around the house. He also decided to radically revamp his business strategy. More and more competition was springing up in the grocery world. But new developments were taking hold in the realm of dry cleaning. My grandfather wanted to give this new business a try.

In 1940 George moved his family to a two-flat house on Leamington Avenue, just around the corner from what would become Supreme Cleaners on Laramie Avenue. Bertha's talent was sewing, so she became the seamstress. George took charge of marketing the new business venture by spreading the word wherever he could. He was also the main fixture at the store counter as he waited on customers. Bertha balanced her seamstress duties with her full-time work of caring for five children still at home.

There is No God, Or Is There?

These were hectic times. Five children and two parents were crammed into a two-bedroom flat. The older children were getting married and starting their families. My grandfather's oldest son, George, wed Mary, moved into the second floor of the Leamington house, and started a family. His first grandchild was born in November of 1941. He was named, appropriately, George.

As my grandfather's children were growing up and moving out of the house, and as grandchildren were being born to him in the 1940's, he and his new wife decided that they wanted more children, too. In 1948 they had a bouncing baby boy, Richard. Then in 1951 they celebrated the birth of a daughter, Bonnie. My grandfather was now the father of ten. Money was tight and life was non-stop, but he was happy again.

Supreme Cleaners became rooted in the community. Business was steady and provided a reasonable income for my grandfather. He even taught two of his sons how to open their own dry cleaning stores. The Hides entrepreneurial spirit lived on. My grandfather's oldest son went into the restaurant business and opened George's Grill just down the street from my grandfather's store. I loved to stop by the Grill with my parents to sit on the green vinyl stools at the counter, sip a cool soda, and eat a delicious cheeseburger. The fruit of my grandfather's labors were finally coming to light. After fifty years of hard work, sweat, trial, and toil, his influence and impact were flourishing. He had come a long way since he stepped onto Ellis Island in the first decade of the 1900's. When he passed his seventy-fifth birthday, his youngest daughter was getting ready to get out of high school, his youngest son was

Chapter Three

close to graduating from Northwestern University, he had thirty-four grandchildren, and a brand new future was emerging for him and Bertha. They would have an empty nest! They would be able to take new steps personally and in business. More adventures were waiting.

In addition to family developments, the relationships in the neighborhood blossomed. Supreme Cleaners was a steady presence for the people of the area. Times were changing and stores were closing, but George refused to leave a neighborhood that had been his home since he arrived in the United States. His family had settled there, and his friends and customers counted on him.

But on April 22, 1970, everything would change. Early that morning, three young men made their way to Chicago from Ohio. Along their meandering path, they had robbed stores, stolen liquor, and fueled their random rampage with drugs. They landed in Chicago with weapons ready. Their mission was to find another target. And they found one shortly after noon at 429 North Laramie Avenue.

Chapter Three Discussion Questions:
Rebuilding

1. George expected life to go fairly smoothly. Why do loss and tragedy surprise us so much?

2. You may have experienced hurt or loss that wounded you deeply. What thoughts and feelings surface when the wind is knocked out of you by bad events?

3. George sent most of his children away after his wife died. Think about an extreme sacrifice in your life. Why did you make it and how did you get through it?

4. Joy came back into George's life. Is life completely random, swinging back and forth from joy to sadness, or, in your opinion, is there order and purpose to life?

5. How do you expect your life to turn out? Give specific details.

6. How might these expectations run up against some unexpected realities? How do you anticipate you will respond?

Chapter Four
Destruction

Ω

Two men waited outside as one entered my grandfather's store. It was broad daylight, but the men were emboldened by the desire for more cash. As the gunman entered the store, he saw my grandfather's friend, Nick, sitting in a chair in the far right corner of the store lobby. My grandfather stood behind the counter directly next to the cash register. The young man stepped inside, looked quickly at Nick and back at my grandfather, brandished his pistol, and told my grandfather to give him the money from the cash register.

My grandfather paused for a moment. Part of him wanted to calm the situation down. The armed man was edgy and agitated. Perhaps the situation could be diffused. Another part of my grandfather wanted to plan a defense. He did not want this brash intruder to succeed. My grandfather worked for years to earn what he had. How could he allow an impulsive thug to take what was rightfully his? This wasn't right. It wasn't the way it was supposed to be. There had to be a way to repel this poor excuse for a man, a person who would rather steal than work hard and earn his keep.

So, my grandfather looked at the knife he had hidden behind the counter. He put it there because the neighborhood had experienced some robberies. The area was more dangerous than it was before. My grandfather wanted to be able to defend himself. The knife was for some extra security--just in case. So he looked at the hidden weapon and thought for just a moment how he might drive the intruder away. But the pause must have alarmed the nervous robber. Suddenly startled, the man raised his gun and fired. The bullet tore through my grandfather's chest and blasted through his back. My grandfather was shocked. He clutched his bleeding chest and fell to the floor.

The gunman ran to the cash register, opened the drawer and grabbed all the money. It was a total of twenty-five dollars. Nick sat stunned in his chair, trying to catch a glimpse of George behind the counter. The robber ran from the store and escaped into the streets with his two accomplices. Nick sprang into action. He dashed to George and saw him bleeding on the floor. Bolting out the door, he ran down the street to George's Grill where Bertha was having lunch with my grandfather's son, George, and his wife Mary. They couldn't believe what they heard from Nick. Immediately, George called the police. The foursome then ran back to the dry cleaners to try to help.

My grandfather lay there, gasping for breath. A pool of blood was growing larger on the floor beneath him. His wife, his first-born son, his daughter-in-law, and his good friend gathered around him. His son worked to stop the bleeding while my grandmother held his hand and stroked his forehead. With a frantic voice, Nick tried to explain what happened. Tears flowed from Bertha and Mary's eyes. Sirens soon wailed in the background and swelled in volume as they drew closer to the dry cleaning shop. A crowd gathered outside. My grandmother

Chapter Four

wondered if her husband was going to die on the floor of his own store in a pool of his own blood.

The ambulance arrived along with the police. The paramedics rushed inside and began to work on George. The crowd outside grew larger and louder. The activity inside became a frenzied blur of medical commotion, tears, and intense conversation. Soon, my grandfather was loaded into the ambulance, Bertha and Mary by his side. Nick and George stayed behind to talk with the police.

This was a nightmare. As the ambulance siren wailed, my grandmother thought about everything she and my grandfather had been through. They had weathered so many storms. They had come through such difficult obstacles. It wasn't supposed to end like this. He wasn't supposed to die yet.

Once they reached the hospital, the doctors rushed my grandfather into surgery. As my grandmother huddled in the waiting room, Mary started to make phone calls. It didn't take long for the family to start arriving. Shocked sons, daughters, in-laws, and grandchildren began to gather. Tears, hugs, and conversation filled the waiting room.

When I arrived home from school that day, my mother broke the news to my brothers and me. My grandfather had been shot in a store robbery. He was in the hospital and was alive, but in serious condition. They didn't catch the robber yet.

I couldn't believe what I heard. My grandfather, *my grandfather,* had been shot. I was young, but the intrusion of this violent act shook me to the core. This was not right. A stranger stepped into our lives and violently assaulted someone we loved. Now we were left hanging in fear, doubt and sadness, and he was somewhere out there.

If you've ever experienced the violent suffering of a loved one, you understand the agonizing thoughts that creep into your consciousness. Was he afraid? What did he feel as the gun went off? How painful was this? What anguish did he endure? The thoughts can be torturous.

I waited at home with my brothers while my mother and father went to the hospital. They returned home later that evening with the news that my grandfather made it through surgery. He was still alive.

With my grandfather recovering in the hospital, my parents sent us to school the next day. I was angry. As I shared the news with my classmates, I suddenly felt the strong desire to see the man who shot my grandfather punished. What right did he have to do this? How could he get away with it?

A few days later the three robbers were found and arrested. One of the police officers at the scene of the arrest was the husband of one of my cousins--one of George's granddaughters. Word had it that the criminal was made to feel very sorry that he stepped into my grandfather's store. I was glad to hear it.

As my grandfather lay in the hospital, various family members kept vigil for him there. Shifts of sons, daughters, and their spouses sat with my grandmother. The bullet had missed

Chapter Four

my grandfather's heart by a fraction of an inch. The wound, however, caused a great deal of damage, traumatizing my grandfather's body. Although his stubborn Greek disposition wouldn't give up easily, his physical resources were stretched. Twenty-six days after my grandfather was gunned down, his body gave out. He couldn't recover. On May 18, 1970 George P. Hides died. Life was stolen from him and from all of us through a random and senseless act of violence that realized a net gain of twenty-five dollars.

It wasn't supposed to happen this way. Life isn't designed to be torn away from you. At least I didn't think it was. The darkness of violent loss adds layers of rage, fear, and emptiness to grief. Heart and mind are tormented along with being saddened. Words cannot describe the anguish and absolute helplessness.

One of the last memories I had of my grandfather was from a recent visit to his house. My grandfather greeted us more joyfully than I had ever experienced. I can still picture him at the entrance of his dining room, throwing his arms open wide as if he was welcoming long-lost relatives. He uttered a loud and gruff shout of welcome as we approached him. Then he did something that completely surprised me. He gave me a dollar. A dollar! A hard-earned dollar--like the one framed in his store. He joyfully placed it in my hand, patted me on the head, and sent me off to play.

I was thrilled about this act of love and affirmation. I was no longer just a little kid. My grandfather noticed me and invested himself in me. A new season of life with him was starting. There was much to look forward to. But, suddenly, all of that was taken away. Instead of looking into my grandfather's eyes to see a growing relationship and understanding, I was looking into his coffin at a dead, numbing, and tragic end.

His funeral was the first I had experienced. The room at the funeral home was quiet, but filled with muffled sobs. My grandmother was strong for her children and grandchildren. She explained to me that it looked like grandpa was just sleeping. He had a Greek icon nestled into the crook of his elbow. He wore a suit. One hand was on top of the other. My grandmother touched his hands and kissed his forehead. He was cold.

At the church, the Greek Orthodox priest waved incense and spoke a language I couldn't understand. There were wails and tears. At the cemetery, the casket hung over a hole in the ground and was lowered into the earth as grieving bodies bent over in pain and sobs. Leaving the cemetery was difficult for everyone. The magnetic force of finality seemed to immobilize us, making us unable to depart. After plodding steps to our cars, the family left Oakridge cemetery and went to a restaurant for the post-funeral meal.

With nearly seventy immediate family members alone, we actually took over a restaurant. Young and old gathered around the tables. An abundance of food was served. I noticed how strange it was that laughter replaced tears as the family sat together and ate together on this day of sadness. Flowers from the funeral home were brought to the restaurant, their scent

Chapter Four

mixing with the aroma of the meal. My grandmother's oldest sons sat on each side of her, attending to her needs, offering comfort, and telling stories that brought a smile to her face.

Then it was over. My grandmother went home with her college-age son and teenage daughter. Each of us went back to our lives. The gathering of family provided temporary relief. Now we faced normal life with an abnormal intrusion of pain and loss.

For some reason, after I had returned to school, my teacher brought up the issue of the death penalty as we discussed current events. Anger welled up in me as I declared that I was all for it. But I knew that nothing would bring my grandfather back. I was straining against emptiness that could not be filled.

My grandmother went back to the dry cleaners. She picked up where my grandfather had left off. She stood where his blood once covered the floor and operated the business in the neighborhood that took life from her. She carried on. But not for long.

Chapter Four Discussion Questions:
Destruction

1. Pain, evil, and tragedy happen every day. Why do they seem like intrusions--unanticipated interruptions--to the way life is "supposed to be"?

2. Discuss what the real nature of life is with regard to experiencing good and evil.

3. Some people say that all people are "basically good." Discuss whether you agree or disagree with that statement.

4. How do the presence and actions of other people provide genuine help during times of difficulty?

5. What is your opinion about the death penalty? Explain your position.

6. How have you been helped effectively by someone else when you were hurting or disillusioned? Talk about what helped you most.

Chapter Five
Change

Ω

The kids would not let her stay there. By the end of the summer, Bertha's brood of concerned children refused to tolerate another day of life in the old neighborhood. It was too dangerous. The memories were too burdensome. It was not good for their mom. It was time to move. But fifty-five-year-old Bertha was not ready to give up the business.

George and Jack began to search for a new location for Supreme Cleaners. They found a storefront on Irving Park Road in the near northwest suburb of Schiller Park. The place was an old restaurant that needed some work. But it was in a prime location and could be perfect for what Bertha needed. The cleaners would be in the front portion of the space while a living area would be in the back. There would be no commute, no walking through streets that had become dangerous, no memories of death and hurt.

The family sprang into action. They put both the house on Leamington and the store on Laramie up for sale. They signed the contract on the new location and rallied the family together for a renovation party. Swarms of family members descended upon the new property in Schiller Park. It became a beehive of activity. The building was gutted and transformed. A beautiful old ceiling was all that remained of the original structure once the work was done. Soon, a neon sign hung in the window letting the world know that this was now "Supreme Cleaners." The front of the store was spacious and attractive. A large customer waiting area was complemented by a generous space for mending along with a long service counter. There was plenty of room for clothes racks and storage. The new place was beautiful.

It was also Bertha's new home. Part of the former restaurant dining area was walled off and transformed into a spacious living room. Up a couple of stairs and through a door was a kitchen and dining room. Two bedrooms and a bathroom completed the living area. Everyone was in on the renovation. I remember watching my dad retile the bathroom. I hauled boxes of old tile to the garbage as dozens of family members busied themselves with building, painting, and remodeling.

By November of 1970, the new store was ready and the old store was sold. Supreme Cleaners was now in Schiller Park. The Chicago neighborhood that defined my family's life for decades was left behind as a new beginning took hold. The family was happy about the new location. It was much closer to where many of the kids had settled and it was a fresh start. Everyone helped my grandmother make the move to the new place. Business started off briskly. The change was complete.

That year, everyone gathered at my grandmother's new home to celebrate Thanksgiving. It was fun to wander into the store when it was closed. My brothers and I walked through the rows of freshly cleaned, plastic sheathed clothing. We looked out the expansive plate glass windows and watched traffic whiz by. Sometimes my grandmother would unlock the front door so

Chapter Five

we could stroll to Orange Drugs next door or to the bowling alley a couple of doors down.

Behind the counter in her store, she kept a box of toys and a stack of board games from her old house in Chicago. The living area of the new place was appointed with the furniture from the old house. My grandfather's recliner was in one corner with the television directly across the room. A sectional sofa curved around the room and the thick Chicago Tribune lay on the coffee table.

The men usually hung out in the living area as the news or some type of sports game blared from the television. The ladies crowded into the kitchen and dining area. They busied themselves with all the meal preparation and cleanup as they visited and caught up on the latest family news.

On that Thanksgiving, the first since my grandfather was killed, both sides of my family gathered together. My Grandma and Grandpa Newman joined in the holiday festivities. Usually we alternated holiday gatherings with each side of the family, but this was a different year with different circumstances. The family wanted to rally around my grandmother as she felt the sting of a holiday without her husband and as she ventured into the uncharted territory of life in this new place. I remember how different it was to see my Grandpa Newman sitting in my Grandpa Hides' chair.

Both of us sat in the living room. We were alone--not an easy feat in such a large family--and I began to complain. I was angry that everything had to change. My attitude was sour

There is No God, Or is There?

as I sat in an unfamiliar place. My heart ached that my grandfather was gone. Everyone was putting on a happy face and making the best of the situation. My family was trying to be strong for my grandmother, but I hated it. My grandfather was stolen from us. We shouldn't have been in this situation. Our lives should not have been intruded on so violently and unfairly. Why did this have to happen? It didn't. It was senseless. It was absolutely unnecessary. It was wrong. It was painful. And I was mad.

I wondered, as I continued my venting, why god didn't do something. Why didn't he step in? Surely, if he existed, he was watching every step unfold. What kind of god would he be if he lost track of the details or couldn't keep up with the fast pace of the world? What kind of god would stand by and watch such hatred and violence? If he was any kind of god at all, wouldn't he prevent such suffering and pain? What kind of god lets such horrible things happen?

Maybe there was no god. Perhaps he didn't exist. Maybe the myth of god was invented to prop up weak minds that couldn't face reality. Maybe he was a ruse, a smokescreen to control the minds of people who finally saw the truth and wouldn't stand for it.

On that Thanksgiving Day, I was feeling what so many had felt before and what too many others would experience in the future. I was feeling abandoned and betrayed. I was feeling ignored. At the time of my grandfather's greatest need, of our family's greatest need, heaven was silent.

Chapter Five

I joined the ranks of many sufferers crying out at the silence and inactivity of god. Many a parent has watched a precious child suffer and die. Children have grasped for hope and help as they endured cruel and horrendous abuse. The innocent have been slaughtered or have been left to waste away and die. Evil has prevailed over the defenseless. Disasters have overtaken and crushed the lives of countless numbers of people. Every day, pain and loss run rampant. Does god ever speak up or show up?

Many years later, during a trip to Africa as an adult, I would meet a young woman from the United Kingdom. She was there helping to educate Africans during the growing AIDS crisis. The woman recalled how, as a young girl, she asked her priest a simple question about god. She was expressing innocent curiosity. The priest replied harshly that she had no business asking questions. He would tell her what she needed to know and believe. Her job was to be quiet and learn. The woman wondered what kind of god couldn't handle questions. She concluded that it could only be a god invented by men. From that day, she walked away from god and the chatter about him so she could make a real difference in the world.

As I sat in my grandmother's living room in November of 1970, I felt like I was at that point. I was taught to believe that god existed, but I was ready to walk away. When god did nothing the day a murderer pulled the trigger and shot my grandfather, perhaps it showed that there was no god to do anything. Either he didn't care or he didn't exist. Either way, I didn't want any part of such apathetic inactivity. I could do much better on my own.

There is No God, Or is There?

I must have been ranting out loud because my Grandpa Newman gently interrupted me. I had tears in my eyes and was staring at the thick newspaper on the coffee table. I didn't make eye contact with him. I couldn't. He was sitting in my grandfather's chair. The chair was covered with a yellowed bedspread with fringe on its edges. It was a vivid reminder of who was missing and how his absence came about.

My Grandpa Newman said, "Michael, I want to show you something."

He took out a stack of old photographs I had never seen before. I walked toward him and sat on the floor in front of the chair. He began to pass the photographs to me one by one. They were pictures from early in his life.

My Grandpa Newman, like my Grandpa Hides, was born in 1894. Benjamin James Newman was the son of a Chicago police officer and bartender. When Benny, as people called my Grandpa, was just a young boy, his father, John, was shot and killed in the line of duty. Not long after the death of his father, his mother, Martha, remarried--once again to another police officer and bartender. This man, Mr. Koepke, adopted my grandfather, but my grandfather kept the name of his biological father.

Grandpa Newman served in World War I. The pictures were from those days and the days after he returned from his military duty in France. First, Grandpa Newman showed me a picture of him and my grandma. How young they looked! My grandma, Amy Newman, was dressed in typical 1920's flapper

Chapter Five

style. Benny Newman met Amy Alberg after the war. They married in 1923, but lived out some exciting adventures before they settled down. One photo showed them standing in front of an old automobile, a slick looking roadster. My grandpa described how they had to put the cloth top up and button up the side flaps to stay warm during winter driving--especially as they ferried illegal booze up to Fox Lake during prohibition.

Next, he showed me a picture of himself during the war. He was at an airfield and several biplanes were in the background. He talked about how the pilots would drop bombs by hand as they leaned over the side of the plane. Once, an enemy bomber dropped an explosive and blew the tailgate off the truck he was driving. It was a close call.

Then he showed me his truck. There he was, in his wool uniform, standing at attention in front of a massive vehicle. The wheels and tires of the truck were muddy. The ground seemed wet and the leafless trees behind him revealed a damp and bleak winter.

Finally, my Grandpa Newman pulled another photo from the stack, looked into my eyes, and said, "Michael, I heard what you were saying and I understand what you're feeling. That's why it's very important that I show you this picture."

The edge of the photograph was pinched between his thumb and forefinger. He looked at it and looked back at me.

"This, Michael, is a picture of a miracle."

Chapter Five Discussion Questions:
Change

1. What causes you to question god's existence most?

2. What doubts about the order and sensibility of the world hit you as you experience the reality of the world each day?

3. Karl Marx said, "Religion is the opiate of the people." What may be true or false about that statement?

4. How might "religion" be distinct from "god"?

5. Discuss whether or not god is for weak-minded people.

6. Why is the existence of god such a hotly debated issue?

Benjamin J. Newman

Chapter Six
A Miracle

Ω

After declaring war on Germany in April of 1917, the United States congress passed the Selective Service Act the following month. All males between the ages of twenty-one and thirty years of age were to report to local draft boards. Eventually, 2.8 million men would be drafted to serve in World War I. Benjamin James Newman was one of those men. He reported for military duty in Chicago, Illinois on February 25, 1918.

Benny claimed "chauffer" as his occupation. He may have been thinking of the illegal hooch he was chauffeuring out of Chicago, but his stated line of work was parlayed into a more desirable role in his military service. Upon reporting for duty, the sergeant in charge asked that anyone who could drive a truck should step forward. The military was becoming a mechanized force and trucks were emerging as the primary form of transport. In less than a decade, the number of trucks in the United States Military would expand from a dozen to tens of thousands. Trucks were one of the latest, high-tech innovations of military progress, and the army needed drivers. Benny stepped forward.

He never drove a truck before, but taking the chance on trying made sense to him. Benny heard about the brutal trench warfare in Europe. Anything he could do to avoid fighting from a dirty and dangerous hole in the ground appealed to him. Benny was shipped to Florida for training. By June of 1918 he was one of the ten thousand troops per day being sent to France.

My grandpa told me stories about some of his experiences in France during the war. He and his buddies manipulated the ration system so they could get extra bread from French bakeries. He and his fellow truck drivers removed the speed limiting devices from their engines so they could move faster than regulations called for. He also had a few harrowing encounters with the enemy. And he saw his share of devastation.

After the signing of the armistice with Germany on November 11, 1918, Benny was assigned to battlefield cleanup duty. The task was gruesome. My grandfather told me about the time he kicked an army helmet and a human head rolled out. The horror of war left a strong and indelible impression on him. By the summer of 1919, however, troops were being sent home. Benny touched U.S. soil again on July 27, 1919. On August 5th of that year, Corporal Benjamin J. Newman was honorably discharged from the United States Army.

But one experience in France never left him. It was the event captured by the photograph he held in his hand. It was, as he said, the picture of a miracle.

One day, my grandfather recounted, he was transporting a variety of items from the battlefield to disposal areas. Sometimes his truck would be packed with loads of

Chapter Six

German military gear. Sometimes it would be filled with junk from trenches. At other times, unexploded ammunition would be transported to safe areas to be destroyed. After delivering a load, Benny steered his three-ton truck down a slick French cobblestone street. Recent rain and snow made the going a bit more precarious, but he forged ahead, trying to accomplish all he was assigned that day. Driving his truck had become routine. He was good at it and he took pride in the way he could maneuver the massive vehicle to accomplish what he wanted.

As he approached an intersection, he pressed his brake pedal, but the brakes didn't respond. The intersection was a "T" junction with a road to the right and left, but a steep drop-off into a river straight ahead. As his truck barreled forward, Benny stomped on the brakes desperately. There was no time to downshift to slow the truck. The drop-off rushed toward him as he frantically tried to control the vehicle. Suddenly the brakes locked up. The wheels skidded across the cobblestone street and over the edge of the embankment. My grandfather closed his eyes and braced himself for impact. This probably was it for him. If he survived the crash of the truck down the steep drop-off, he knew he wouldn't last in the icy and swift waters below.

Suddenly it was quiet. My grandfather opened his eyes and saw that he didn't plunge into the river. There was no crash. He looked around and saw that his truck was dangling over the deep gorge below. The front of the truck was suspended in mid-air. The back was still on the ground. He didn't move.

There is No God, Or is There?

The silence was broken by shouts of villagers rushing to his aid. Wide-eyed in disbelief, they clamored around and beckoned to him to get out of the truck. Stretching arms, broom handles, and anything they had, they helped my grandfather escape the open cab and brought him to dry land.

No one could believe what had happened. The hulking vehicle, empty of any load, clearly with its weight toward the front, hung over the river without falling. Villagers were so completely astonished that, after making sure my grandfather was okay, they ran to get a photographer to capture the amazing sight on film.

And that is the photograph my grandfather held in front of me. I looked into his sparkling blue eyes as he said, "Michael, this is impossible. It is a miracle."

That was the consensus in the village, too. Not one person there could find a reasonable explanation for what happened. Everyone called it a miracle. After the photo was taken, my grandfather had to convince the villagers to call for military personnel to help pull the truck back onto the road so he could get back to his base. They didn't want to move it. They wanted to stare in amazement and show all their friends and family.

"Michael," my grandfather said, "I know you are hurting very deeply and I know you are very angry, but I am showing you a picture of the impossible. I am showing you something that is miraculous. It runs counter to all natural laws. It is not natural. It is supernatural."

Chapter Six

He went on, "If you're going to write god off, you have to consider this. You have to ask how it happened and what it means."

I did not expect this from my Grandpa Newman. By this time in his life he was seventy-six years old. He was bald, had a pretty good size gut on him, and never ever appeared to be the assertive or confrontational type. In fact, he was a very quiet man. His typical pose during our visits was to sit in his favorite chair at home, drink a highball--a mixture of whiskey and ginger ale, and watch the Chicago Cubs on television. During most of our family visits to his house in River Grove, Illinois, I never heard him say a word. Suddenly, in a different context, my grandpa became very verbal and demonstrative. The photographs fascinated me. The stories held me in rapt attention. The challenge to my ranting was startling.

I decided to challenge back.

"Why didn't Grandpa Hides get a miracle? Why did god let him be killed?"

"I don't know," my Grandpa Newman replied. "But it's important for you to realize that your tragedy and hurt aren't proof that god doesn't exist."

My grandfather was a common man. He was a laborer all his life. He didn't hang around with highbrow academics or read philosophy in his spare time. But he knew what he knew. He had seen plenty. He was not a naïve newcomer to the human race. He also wasn't a religious man. He wasn't against it necessarily, but he didn't go to church or get involved in religious practices. He was a regular, ordinary guy. But today he was a guy who was staunchly advocating for the supernatural. He knew what he knew.

Holding up the picture, he said, "There's more to this life than just you and me and here and now. Something is out there. Someone is out there."

I didn't want to argue with my grandfather, but I had to say something. I couldn't brush off my deep pain and the unfair theft of my other grandfather's life.

"But I don't understand," I said. "It doesn't make sense. What kind of god would let something so wrong happen?"

At the time, I didn't have a clue about the depth of this question. I had no idea about the suffering taking place around the world. I was ignorant of the injustice, the chaos, and the random turmoil of loss, victimization, and violence hurting life after life. I wasn't aware that even those who claimed to be religious were some of the worst culprits of meanness and inflicting pain. I just knew it was all senseless and unfair.

My grandfather responded, "Maybe you can't understand. Maybe you'll never understand. If you did," he paused to look at the picture in his hand, "maybe it wouldn't be supernatural at all. Maybe god wouldn't be god. He would just be you."

I was not feeling good about this conversation. I shot back, "Well, maybe you just don't know how bad this feels. Maybe you don't care either."

Chapter Six

My grandfather sat back in the chair. He took a deep breath. I could see the hurt in his eyes, but I could also see that he wasn't backing down.

"My seven-year-old daughter died of pneumonia as I held her in my arms. I saw your grandmother's beautiful blond hair turn white because of her grief. The day you were born, Michael, Grandma Newman was in surgery for breast cancer. I didn't know whether she would live or die. But along with the reality of devastating pain, there is the reality of the miraculous. What are you going to do with that? You can't really deny one or the other can you? One doesn't really disprove the other, does it?"

I didn't know what to say. I remembered my dad mentioning the sister he never knew. Ruth was her name. I remembered the story of how my grandmother's hair turned white as she grieved the loss of her little girl. My grandma was in her twenties. It crushed her. I didn't know about her surgery the day I was born.

I sat there stewing, suddenly lacking any conclusions.

Chapter Six Discussion Questions:
A Miracle

1. In your opinion, is the supernatural real?

2. Share and discuss any unexplained events or miracles you have experienced.

3. If you have witnessed something unexplainable, what does it tell you about the reality of life in this world?

4. Benjamin Newman asserted that tragedy and hurt do not prove that god doesn't exist. Discuss why you agree or disagree with this claim.

5. Benjamin Newman also stated, "Something is out there. Someone is out there." Discuss your thoughts about this statement.

6. If god exists, what, in your opinion, should he be doing in this world?

Chapter Seven
Proof

Ω

"It's difficult to argue with, isn't it?"

My Grandpa Newman held the photograph of him standing in front of his truck as it teetered over the river's edge. He stood next to the empty truck bed, a surprised smile on his face. The heavy cab hung over empty space. The wet cobblestone street spread beneath his feet and the river stretched out into the background, a bridge visible toward the horizon.

"But why do such terrible things happen?" I said to him with tears.

"Like I said," he replied, "I don't know. But all of the terrible things that happen--like your Grandpa Hides' death--prove that this world can be a painful place, a deeply painful place with evil, tragedy, and a lot of hurt. It all proves that we have a very deep need."

"What do we need?" I asked.

"We need help."

"Well, we aren't getting much, are we?" I shot back.

All of this bothered me. Who would allow such a chaotic and broken existence? It made no sense. It was completely random. No god could be a part of this kind of mess. Anyone who thought so had to be delusional or very weak-minded.

Later in my life I would read authors who asserted that belief in god was a crutch, an opiate that helped them deal with the stark reality of a pain-filled, broken world. Surely my own grandfather wouldn't be retreating into claims of the supernatural to escape reality! I couldn't be related to that kind of muddy thinking!

Grandpa Newman spoke up. "You may be getting more help than you realize."

He spoke firmly, but I could tell he cared about how I felt.

He went on. "Michael, I can't prove anything about god and I don't have to. It's not my job to defend him and he doesn't need me or anyone else to do that. God will prove himself if he wants to. You just have to pay attention."

My grandpa looked at the picture of his miracle. Clearly, this was not a tool of denial or escape. This wasn't a crutch in his life. It was a fact. It was a real occurrence that was unexplainable. It was something supernatural that intruded into his life and showed him that there was something more than the here and now. I couldn't take that fact away from his life. I didn't want to. But a feeling of unfairness welled up inside of me. If the supernatural happens randomly to some and not others, what was that all about? Was god a cruel jokester playing with the lives of helpless humans? Was he mean? Were we at the mercy of a powerful supernatural being who toyed with our emotions or absentmindedly zapped a select group of people with supernatural help?

I mumbled to my grandfather, "Maybe god just doesn't care about me. Maybe he hates me."

"Or, maybe the fact that your deep pain causes you to rage against him is the way he shows you that he is real. You're not the center of the universe, Michael. All of life doesn't cater to your needs and work to insure your happiness. The world is a much bigger place than that. But in some way, at some time, you will run into the supernatural, the miraculous, and the unexplainable. You will cross paths with god, just like you are doing now. Like I said, he will prove himself. He will confront you in some way and you will have to deal with him."

I tried to distance myself from the conversation "Well, I don't care. I just don't care. I don't need to think about the supernatural, god, or any spiritual stuff," I said. "It doesn't matter anyway."

"That's exactly the way it was when I went to war," my grandpa continued. "I was twenty-four years old. Chicago was an exciting place. Everything was changing. People were caught up in new technology and new ideas. Even though the war was raging overseas, we were having a great time here at home. Everyone loved sports stars and movie stars. Every night, you could find a place to have fun. There was dancing, movies, drinking, and friends. We used to go to Riverview Park in Chicago. It was an amusement park with a ride called "The

There is No God, Or is There?

Bobs," one of the best roller coasters ever. I didn't have much money, but I didn't have a care in the world. All I really cared about was me. I was living the single life and having a great time."

I always enjoyed hearing stories about the "old days." Sometimes it was hard to believe that there was a time my grandpa was young and carefree. He could tell he had my attention.

He went on. "My friends were just like me. It wasn't that life was a constant party. We cared about people and we cared about the world. That's one reason I was fine with joining the army. I wanted to do my duty and to help in any way I could. But god never really fit in anywhere. He was a non-factor. He didn't matter."

As I listened, I realized that I still cared. I was mad at god. I was angry that he--if there was a "he" at all--let my Grandpa Hides die a horrible and frightening death. I didn't realize that I was living during a time very similar to the early 1900s. The 1960s had barely transitioned into 1970. A man had walked on the moon in technological triumph, but the country was torn apart by protests and turmoil. People were deeply concerned about making a difference in the world, but they were disillusioned with the institutional establishment. In many circles, god was being viewed as irrelevant at best, and a contrived and destructive tool of religious power-mongers at worst. Indifference to god took hold as activists sought meaning in life apart from the old structures of society. People wanted purpose in life, but they saw it in relevant and hands-on

Chapter Seven

acts of kindness to other people. From their perspective, the religious establishment was a place for political maneuvering and social oppression. The god of traditional institutionalism was a non-factor, meaningless. People needed to do what mattered. They needed to help the oppressed and to fight for what was right.

Others during that era simply wanted to indulge in what was forbidden and to dispose of old structures. It was a confusing time, a purifying time, and a corrupt time. And it was pretty close to what my Grandpa Newman experienced during his younger days. As America approached the roaring twenties, my grandfather's indifference toward god typified the spirit of many young people from metropolitan areas like Chicago.

My grandfather continued to reflect. "I suppose I had good reason to be angry with god. My dad was killed. We were uprooted as a family. My mom got remarried. But I didn't get angry. I just didn't think about any of it. I went my own way and was indifferent to spiritual things. God wasn't even on my radar. Maybe that's why I was so surprised during the war. I discovered something about god: if you don't care about him, he may surprise you by chasing you down. Even in your indifference, god pursues you."

Two things shocked me about this conversation. First, this was the longest conversation I ever had with my grandpa. He never took time to show me pictures or to reveal things about his past. This was a new experience for me. I saw a side of him that I had never seen before. The second shocking part of this interaction with my grandpa was that he didn't seem

There is No God, Or is There?

threatened or defensive at all. He was completely at ease with my assertion that god did not exist. My grandfather wasn't threatened by the fact that even if god did exist, I didn't care. At that time in my life, any opposition to an adult or to an established idea would earn me a harsh rebuke or a slap on the mouth. Exchanging ideas and dialoging about the deeper questions of life weren't exactly what kids did with adults back then. My grandfather displayed a quiet and comfortable confidence in two key ideas: we can't prove god exists, but god will prove that he exists; even if we don't care about god, he will pursue us.

My grandfather handed me the small stack of photographs from the war and from his early days with my grandmother. I flipped through them and was mesmerized by these images from the past. One picture showed my grandpa sitting on some padded wicker furniture. It was a staged photograph with a painted island backdrop behind him and some genuine palm branches next to him. He looked dapper in his military uniform, young and clean cut. No doubt, it was a photo he had taken in France. Maybe he sent it home to family.

Part of me had forgotten about the pain and grief I was feeling when we first started talking. But as I looked at the photos it all came rushing back. I handed the stack back to my grandpa, walked to the couch, and plopped down on it with a deep sigh.

My grandfather spoke up. "It's not easy to go through terrible things, but it's not easy to go through good things, either. Sometimes the terrible things help you in life more than

Chapter Seven

the good things. Bad times shape you and usually bring out the best in the people around you--at least for a while. When good things happen, you can get complacent and careless, and people around you can get ugly. After my truck didn't crash into the river, I saw that firsthand. People got ugly."

I gave a puzzled look at my grandfather and said, "What do you mean? What did people do?"

"If I would have died, I would have been considered a military hero," he said. "But because I lived and had pictures of what happened, my life got miserable fast."

Chapter Seven Discussion Questions:
Proof

1. Benjamin Newman linked an unexplainable event in his life to the existence of god. Discuss whether you feel that this is a fair conclusion.

2. If a supposed god is truly god, how capable would we as humans be to understand or evaluate him?

3. Give your opinion about the statement: "God will prove himself if he wants to. You just have to pay attention."

4. What is your opinion about the pursuit and discussion of spiritual matters?

5. Give your opinion about the statement: "Even in your indifference, god pursues you."

6. Discuss whether good times or bad times shape your character more.

Chapter Eight
Assault

Ω

Benny Newman had to make a full report about what happened along that riverbank. Calling for help to retrieve his truck from its precarious perch required him to complete the appropriate military forms for his superiors. He had to write an account of what took place. He even had to attach a copy of the photo along with names of some of the eyewitnesses. But by simply telling the story, Corporal Benjamin Newman began to get some pushback.

"You're an idiot, Newman," a fellow Motor Transport Corps member told him. "What kind of make-believe stories are you telling?"

The early 1900s was an age of skepticism and derision toward the supernatural. It was a scientific age, a time of technological advancement and the triumph of human ingenuity. Even in the face of some of the greatest human failures and signs of complete human weakness, a spirit of arrogant indestructibility and unlimited human potential prevailed. The unsinkable ship, Titanic, hit an iceberg on its maiden voyage in 1912 and plunged to the bottom of the ocean. Fifteen hundred passengers were lost. Some on board were the most wealthy and powerful people of that time. But the human vulnerability exposed in that tragic accident did not take root in people's hearts. It was also during that era that

There is No God, Or is There?

World War I raged throughout Europe. The war put human cruelty and fallibility on display for the world. The war came to a fizzling halt as an influenza pandemic swept across the globe, killing millions, weakening armies, and showing that a small germ could cripple a strong and proud society.

But the age of human triumph forged ahead. Even in the midst of war, the supernatural was not always a welcome subject. Even though he wasn't trying to make a big deal of it, Benjamin Newman received his fair share of ridicule. Suddenly, he was accused of being feeble and delusional. It was confusing to Benny. He was simply telling a story. He was reciting facts. But the response was loud and strong in protest and ridicule.

The worst assault, however, took place in a surprising and unexpected way. Time and experience began to eat away at my grandfather and his miracle. He returned from France in July of 1919 and was honorably discharged on August 5th of that year. From that point on, his life hit one obstacle after another.

He and my grandmother married in 1923, but before and after their marriage, my grandfather had trouble establishing a career. He moved from one short-term job to another. For a while he worked in a tin factory. There was no shortage of tinsel in the Newman household at Christmas! He labored six days a week, leaving no time for his beloved fishing. But all of his work landed him nowhere.

The economic crash in 1929 threw him into the turmoil of an unemployed nation. By 1939 he took the Civil Service exam and became one of the first employees on duty at the

Chapter Eight

newly activated Chicago Medical Depot for the Army Service Forces. World War II was reinvigorating employment opportunities for large numbers across the nation. My grandfather advanced to the position of Head Foreman of Laborers and received excellent reviews from his superiors. He secretly supervised German prisoners of war who were put to work by the United States government. My grandfather spoke fluent German and could manage the secret foreigners. But by March of 1946, the end of the war also took its toll on war-related industry and employment. My grandfather was removed from his position due to a reduction in forces. He was nearly fifty-two years old and out of work once again. The market was being flooded with young men fresh out of the military. What would he do now?

Added to his anxiety was the pain caused by his daughter's death. My grandmother was never the same after Ruth died. But they still had two boys to care for. My father was eleven years old when my grandpa lost his job. My dad's brother was fifteen. This was not a time my grandfather could lay back and take it easy. He needed to put food on the table.

It had been twenty-seven years since my grandfather's miracle. What did it all mean? Was it really real? He began to experience what time and trial do to a human being. With time, failures accumulate and the weight of broken dreams grows heavier. Young people live brashly from moment to moment, trusting that the future will fall into place as they hope it will, believing that failures of the moment will be redeemed by new opportunities and successes to come. But looking back from middle age could very well be a view of unrealized dreams and unanticipated wounds from life that didn't always go as planned. Questions creep in. Doubts develop. Could he have done more for Ruth? Did he make the right job decisions? Should he have stuck with school longer? Was he a failure? Why was he in this difficult situation at his age? Why was life regressing instead of progressing? If there was a god, why was he letting life crumble into loss and chaos instead of stepping up with another miracle to show that he was around? Why would god give the impression that the world is spinning out of control? Why does it seem that miraculous help is available at one moment, but emptiness and silence prevail in the next?

My grandpa realized that life means living in the tension of success and struggle, gain and loss, joy and pain. As he saw in the war, complete chaos and the startlingly miraculous coexist at the exact same time. Both experiences are very real. But one does not cancel the other out. His doubt raged, but his miracle was still very real. Each did not disprove the other. Both existed. He experienced the supernatural. He had a picture of it! It was real. He knew there was more to life than the natural world. On the other hand, he experienced the natural world in all its beauty and fury. It was shocking to see the majesty of a misty dawn over the devastation of a desolate battlefield. He witnessed the splendor of sunrises and sunsets while he was in France along with the brutal and ugly deaths of friends and strangers. Yes, the natural world had teased him and had taken its toll over the years. Who can describe the love of a father for his sweet daughter? Who can verbalize the feeling of watching that precious daughter slip away? Who can articulate the pain of not being able to afford a proper funeral

Chapter Eight

during the depression and having his little daughter's body laid in his own home as visitors paid their respects? My grandfather was pulled in two directions. Reasons for doubt and reasons for belief filled the years of his existence. Now jobless and disheartened, he weighed the two as he looked toward the future.

The challenge he faced was to live with both. Pain and loss are ugly and devastating, but he couldn't allow pain and loss to lead him to the denial of the miraculous. Traveling down the road of bitter denial would taint accurate thinking. To assert that the natural world was all we had, that there was no supernatural phenomenon, that there was no possibility of god, that nothing existed beyond us, would be tantamount to my grandfather throwing a tantrum, flailing fists at god because my grandfather did not get his way as often as he would have liked. Scientifically declaring that god did not exist would be to deny facts and observations that were unexplainable by natural means. In other words, it would be unscientific. My grandfather couldn't travel that road of bitterness, denial, and self-deception.

Likewise, he couldn't hide in the miraculous. He couldn't dismiss the horrible pain that plunges people into darkness, the senseless and seemingly random destruction of both the innocent and guilty, or the purposelessness and despair that life brings--that he felt at fifty-two years of age. His experience with the miraculous also could not mask or minimize the corruption of religion or the great harm done in the name of the miraculous. It would be naïve to pretend that everything was okay, that living a Pollyanna existence would make injustice, evil, and hurt disappear. That would be clouded thinking, too.

No, he had to live with both doubt and belief. He had to acknowledge both the natural and the supernatural. He had to hang on to his picture while he muddled through his pain. This was the tension of real life. It was living without all the answers. It was being able to see and understand only a portion of existence. It was living with questions and doubts even as he held onto some answers and certainties.

One thing my grandfather realized at this juncture in his life was that the rigors of living through the years led him to thinking that was deeper than ever. When he was twenty-five he may have been accused of being self-deceiving and idealistic. He was just a kid, after all. He was a young upstart thrown into the turmoil of war. Who wouldn't want to lean on the crutch of the miraculous in order to survive and to dull the pain of war? But entering his fifties and having endured so much, no one could call him an idealistic neophyte. He was asking big questions, facing stark realities, and weighing all the facts. Holding on to the miraculous while at the same time wrestling with doubt indicated sound and honest thinking, a true and credible approach to life. He would neither surrender to bad science nor hide in self-deceiving religion.

My grandfather moved forward steadily, facing the facts. What he needed now was a job. Due to accrued vacation time, he was paid through the end of July 1946. After weeks of searching, handing out letters of recommendation, and hitting one dead end after another, he finally got hired on as a railroad

Chapter Eight

watchman. He worked this job until he retired, two years before I was born.

Benjamin Newman was seventy-six years old when he told me his story and showed me his miracle as we sat in my grandmother's new living room on Thanksgiving Day. He never spoke to me about his encounter with the supernatural again. Our visits resumed their previous form: my family regularly stopped by their humble suburban River Grove house. My brothers and I played with plastic soldiers in the back yard, went to the park across the street, or shot pool in the basement while my grandpa sat in his favorite chair, drank a highball, and quietly watched television. Every now and then I would unearth a relic of the past as I rummaged through boxes in the basement bedroom: one of my grandpa's military patches or a book that belonged to him when he was a kid. But I never saw the stack of photos again. I never again heard him tell the remarkable stories of life during the war or of his early adventures with my grandmother. But I never forgot.

Chapter Eight Discussion Questions:
Assault

1. What do hurt, tragedy, and pain in this world prove?

2. Discuss whether living life really means "living in the tension of success and struggle, gain and loss, joy and pain."

3. How does science deal with the fact of miraculous events?

4. How does science explain tragedy, hurt, and chaos?

5. How has religion caused inaccurate and deluded thinking?

6. What "bad science" have you encountered in both the natural and supernatural areas of thinking?

Chapter Nine
Endings

Ω

Benjamin J. Newman was almost ninety-one years old when he died. The goodbyes started several years before his death when my grandfather began his slow decline into dementia and physical disability. Strokes began to cripple him. Mental capacity faded. Only glimmers of his true self surfaced from time to time.

A few years after our Thanksgiving conversation, his ability to take care of himself and to tend to the needs of his home waned. My grandmother's memory was diminishing, too. My father and his brother took alternating weekly shifts to visit their parents, check on home safety issues, and dispose of spoiling food in the refrigerator. After my grandfather fell once again and couldn't get up even with my grandmother's help, the need for a change was clear. It broke their hearts to sell their home and move to a new senior living center. My grandfather was angry about the move and showed it by clamming up. He refused to talk--unless he was bribed with a highball or he was alone with his grandkids. A series of strokes finally took their toll and he was transferred to an onsite nursing care unit. My energetic grandmother visited him every day as she walked briskly around the facility and greeted everyone she saw. Finally, on July 26, 1985, Benny Newman's heart gave out. His long journey ended.

There is No God, Or is There?

I knew it was the end of an era. Here was a man born in the 1800s, a World War I veteran, a person who was an eyewitness to the dramatic changes of the twentieth century, a living history book. No one could replace him. His kind was dwindling. Here was a man who worked hard in humble jobs, but helped build the nation into the powerhouse of the world. Who could ever see from his perspective? Here was a man who experienced the miraculous and showed me that hope is not lost. Who would carry that message? At the end of his life, the gutsy warrior, the daring bootlegger, the devoted husband and father, the meticulous laborer, had to wear a bib as a nurse fed him. Once again, the decay of natural life rubbed up against the euphoria of a supernatural intrusion. But that was reality.

My grandmother lived for another eighteen years without her beloved Benny. She died just before her 102nd birthday. Her memory was not as sharp, but she motored around at full strength up until a few days before her death in 2003.

It's never easy to lose a loved one, but walking the journey with someone to a peaceful death is much easier than having a loved one violently stolen from you. The wounds of imposed grief are jagged and resistant to healing.

More than a year after my Grandpa Hides' murder, the family finally received word about the killer's trial. The wheels of justice moved very slowly, and the slowness caused my anger to simmer. I hated the person who killed my grandfather. I couldn't believe that the legal system plodded along with what seemed like detached indifference. A man killed my

Chapter Nine

grandfather! It was a heinous and hurtful crime! What was taking so long?

Some details of the trial trickled my way, but I didn't hear very much about what was happening. I was hoping that the murderer would be put to death. That's how I felt. Instead, the man was found guilty and sentenced to prison. It was difficult to live with the fact that the person who stole my grandfather's life would have a future. After grieving for more than a year and seeing some semblance of normalcy begin to take hold, the news of the trial and conviction brought all of my hurt to the surface again. Our whole family relived the grief and pain of my grandfather's death. It was another terrible time. I wondered if life would ever feel right again. I wondered if the anger and sadness would ever surrender their grip on my heart and mind. I learned that it takes years for the soul to rebuild and recover after a violent death shakes it to the core.

Both of my grandfathers were gone. Each was born in the same year. Both experienced great adventure, risk, and romance. Both experienced tremendous loss and heartbreak. Both expressed satisfaction with what life brought them--even in the midst of unspeakable trial and unexpected chaos. One met an untimely and tragic end. The other faded away with no recognition or fanfare.

The lives of these two men converged to teach me much. My Grandpa Hides taught me how short life is and how each moment must be savored. He also taught me that the deep pain of being victimized by violence is a brutal internal battle. Fear, sadness, anger, and pain are blended into a volatile and torturous mix. This concoction flows through the heart, soul, and mind uncontrolled. Time helps dilute its toxic effects. But fending off denial and anger helps neutralize it most.

That is what my Grandpa Newman taught me. He didn't teach this by stirring up my emotions or firing me up to keep going by presenting an inspirational or motivating message. No, he taught me to think, to evaluate, and to be watchful. He presented me with simple and sensible facts that allowed me to avoid being dragged away by self-indulgent thought and self-centeredness.

The first way my grandpa helped keep me from being swallowed up by anger and denial was to let me know that my feelings didn't determine reality. My anger, hurt, and confusion did not define the total actuality of everything that existed around me. Running with my pain into a denial of anything good would be an act of nonsense. Anger with god that led to a denial of the supernatural would be senseless. That principle extended to the anger and pain caused by the institutional church. The corrupt and cruel actions perpetrated by organized religion throughout history did not mean that the supernatural never happened. My grandpa taught me that the existence of both the natural and supernatural world does not depend on my emotions or my opinions. If there is a god, he can take care of himself.

That's the second lesson my grandpa taught me about getting lost in anger or denial. He let me know that god, if he exists, can take care of himself and will, if he is real, take care of

Chapter Nine

proving he's around if he wants to. I don't need to fight against god's existence. I don't need to fight for god's existence. After all, if he is god, why would he need me to defend him? And, if he is god, why would my protests make any difference at all? My grandpa taught me that I could relax about god. I can relax about what I can't understand. I can relax about the miraculous and supernatural. I can't cause the supernatural to happen. I can't activate god. If god is god, he'll make that clear. He'll come to me. My job is to observe reality and draw conclusions based on that reality.

That's the third way my grandpa taught me to live a life balanced by reality. My job wasn't to try to know it all. It was to be attentive in order to learn something. If I refused to pay attention to the facts, I would be sticking my head in the sand. The facts included chaotic, hurtful, crushing, and heartbreaking events in my life. My grandfather made it clear that pain doesn't disprove god; it proves the chaotic reality of life in this world, the deep need each of us has, and the weakness and helplessness that each of us will face at one time or another. The facts also include surprising, unexplainable, serendipitous, astonishing, and unforeseen mysteries that may appear and show us that there is more to life than the natural. Both of these dynamics exist together. I can try to make sense of this dual reality. I can ponder it. I can muse about it. I can rage about it. But what I do will not change the facts. My job is to learn the facts, embrace the facts, and learn how to live well with the facts. This is not fatalism. It is living as one who thinks carefully and who understands that the world is a complex place. I cannot pretend to have a full understanding of the intricate mechanisms of the universe. I cannot deceive myself and believe that I am able to exert my control or authority over those intricacies. My job is to be attentive to every reality and live effectively within those realities.

The fourth way my grandfather taught me to live an effective life, free from the confines of denial and anger, was by teaching me to acknowledge that life is complicated. Everything we experience, observe, and learn points to the fact that life is always more complex than we think. When tragedy strikes, we suddenly realize that life is not what we expected. We're taken on a ride we didn't ask for. We learn things about the world and ourselves that we did not set out to learn. When a miracle happens, we are sent on a journey of joy, surprise, relief, and discovery that we could never imagine or predict.

Every close look at life reveals a new layer of intricacy. Go deeper into the ocean and new creatures are discovered. Develop more complex accelerators and microscopes and new particles beyond the atom are revealed. Study biological functions more carefully and new purpose for body systems and organs are uncovered. Penetrate the universe with more powerful telescopes and new stars and galaxies come into view. Life in this world leads to ever more profound encounters with new complexity. Knowledge and discovery do not counter the existence of the supernatural. Science does not prove that god cannot exist. Knowledge proves that our lives and world are boundless in complexity.

The final lesson my grandfather taught me is that both tragedy and miracles happen to ordinary people. My

Chapter Nine

grandfather was one of the most ordinary people I've ever met. He wasn't famous. He wasn't connected with a renowned crowd. He wasn't an extrovert. He never even raised his voice or showed great enthusiasm about anything. But he experienced both the extraordinary and the tragic in his ordinary life. He saw the worst of what life can bring. He also saw firsthand that there was something more to life than the natural, predictable course of events. Something amazing happened to him. He was a young, uneducated man with a rebellious streak. He wasn't holy or religious. He wasn't a preacher or motivational speaker. He was a regular person. And into his regular life barged terrible experiences. But the miraculous also intruded into his life. That's the way both the natural and supernatural work. It all happens to regular people. At times life will resemble the worst headlines in the news. At other times, the unexplainable will happen when you least expect it. This rhythm will occur in everyone's life. No one will live a life without pain. No one will live life without encountering the unexplainable.

Of course, this doesn't lead to an endorsement of religion. It simply acknowledges the fact that there is more to life than the ordinary, sometimes kind, sometimes cruel course of natural events. There is more. There is mystery. There is miracle. Instead of shutting down and shutting life out after my Grandpa Hides' murder, my Grandpa Newman taught me to keep my eyes open. If I did, I may see the miraculous. I may encounter god.

Chapter Nine Discussion Questions:
Endings

1. What are the hazards of living in the denial of the supernatural?

2. What danger exists in becoming hyper-religious?

3. How would you describe a balanced pursuit of exploring both the natural and supernatural realities of life?

4. Part of the discussion in this chapter is about a realistic view of self in relation to the universe. How might we err in overstating or underestimating our significance and impact?

5. Discuss the statement: "Science does not prove that god cannot exist. Knowledge proves that our lives and world are boundless in complexity."

6. Discuss the statement: "There is more to life than the ordinary, sometimes kind, sometimes cruel course of natural events. There is more. There is mystery. There is miracle."

Chapter Ten
Testing

Ω

In April of 1982 I was completing my junior year in college. My Grandpa Hides was killed twelve years before. My Grandpa Newman's health continued to fail as he neared eighty-eight years of age. The events of my life pushed me to study philosophy. I was deep into my major when I received shocking news. My cousin Terri, a twin daughter of my Aunt Betty and Uncle Tony, had been murdered. I couldn't believe it was happening again.

Terri was one of my favorite cousins. She and her sister, Tina, were fraternal twins. They used to play with my mind as they talked about their twinhood. Terri was blond; Tina was a brunette. Their builds were different. They were different heights. My brothers and I didn't understand how they could be twins! They were six years older than me, but they treated me like a best buddy whenever we visited. Our times together were filled with laughter and fun. For some reason, we clicked. I always looked forward to our visits together. But now, a dark cloud of shock and grief rolled into our lives. The feelings were indescribable. Terri, only twenty-seven years old, was dead.

I was three hundred miles away at school when I received the first phone call, but the details trickled in. Terri and her fiancé were found in her basement apartment in Schiller Park, Illinois. My aunt was puzzled when Terri didn't answer her phone. Finally Aunt Betty decided to go to the apartment to see if anything was wrong. When she arrived, the door was ajar. She entered the apartment to find Terri and her fiancé lying in a pool of blood. Both were shot in the face at close range. It was a gruesome and life-shattering discovery. Terri's own mother stumbled on the unimaginable and unspeakable. I shuddered when I heard what happened. With even more potency than at my grandfather's murder, the feelings of horror, grief, and anger welled up inside me.

Much speculation about the circumstances of their deaths began to swirl among the family. Was this drug related? Was there involvement in other unsavory business? But, ultimately, those questions didn't matter. Whatever the circumstances, my cousin died a horrible death. Who could imagine the fear and dread she experienced moments before the gun exploded in front of her eyes? Who could know what she witnessed and what she felt moments before her life was stolen from her?

Gloom and anguish seeped into the hearts of our family members. Once again, the wind was knocked out of me as I pondered the tragic end of a loved one's life. She was only twenty-seven years old. Her death wasn't the result of a random crime spree. Her killer wanted her dead. Cruelly and coldly, he looked into her eyes as he took her life.

If it was possible to feel worse about the death of someone very precious, I did. Compared to my grandfather's murder, this violent, evil, and chaotic act exposed a deeper and more vicious spirit at work in the world. Too often, I read about

Chapter Ten

the pernicious acts and senseless violence of criminals. Now I felt it. I felt it deep inside. It was beyond comprehension, feeling, and description.

Of course, the questions began to surface again. Why? How can there be a god when he lets things like this happen? Is the world simply a random mess of disorder, taking us on a roller coaster of meaninglessness?

I had just completed a Philosophy of Religion class. Part of the curriculum was to review arguments for the existence of god, proofs put forward by philosophers throughout the ages. I could see clearly that these "proofs" didn't prove anything. Each had glaring weaknesses and was based on the presupposition of god.

The ontological proof for god's existence asserted that if a perfect being can be imagined, if it is logically possible to think of god, then god must exist because existence is part of perfection. To deny existence means that the being would not be perfect. Honestly, I don't know if Anselm, one of the proof's proponents, even understood this so-called proof of God's existence.

The cosmological proof of god's existence claimed that because the universe exists, a first cause of the universe must also exist. This first cause, Thomas Aquinas and others reasoned, must be god. The thinking and reasoning in this argument is at least sensible, but, once again, the existence of god is an assumption. It is human conjecture.

There is No God, Or is There?

The teleological proof for god's existence argued that if the end product--the world--is orderly and complex, then there must be one who ordered it. A watch must have a watchmaker. A design must have a designer. The designer must be god. But this assumption has weaknesses. On one hand, there is much debate about the orderliness of the world. Plenty of chaos exists. If god is the designer, is he flawed? If he is flawed, is he really god? On the other hand, there is a great deal of order in the midst of the chaos. But to assume that the order is the product of a divine being is a leap of faith, not an irrefutable proof.

The moral argument for the existence of god claims that all morality points us to the existence of one who is supremely good. If moral truths such as the value of human life, the respect of personal property, and the virtue of honesty exist, then these truths must flow from the ultimate truth. A supreme being must be responsible for this commonly accepted morality among humans. At least that is what Immanuel Kant and others have asserted over the years. Once again, however, this argument is flawed. Moral goodness has had many common threads but is not as completely standard as this argument assumes. In addition, asserting the necessity of god to make the moral rules is a human assumption, not a proof that god exists.

No one can philosophically coerce someone into acknowledging that god exists. These "proofs" are just a few among a variety of ways people have tried to create an irrefutable argument for god's existence. But they don't work. If they did, the arguments for and against god would have

Chapter Ten

stopped long ago. The assumptions in these proofs overlook the fact that the assertion of god is not simply a philosophical and theoretical proposition. If the existence of god is asserted, it means that someone is out there! It means that someone greater than any of us is involved in the journey we call life. It means that there is something deeply personal at stake. If god is in the mix, is he making a difference? If he makes no difference, what good is he? Why does he matter?

Those are the kinds of questions that arise from a head-on collision with life and death. That is the soul searching that results from the deep wounds and, yes, all the random events and circumstances of existence. When life is disorderly and ugly, when existence is immoral and senseless, can the question of god even be brought into the conversation?

That is when I thought about my Grandpa Newman again. It was just a dozen years ago that he showed me the photograph of his miracle. When I was in the pit of gloom, he taught me something that no philosophy class ever articulated. He taught me that miracles and murder exist side by side. Doubt and certainty walk hand in hand on the pathway of life. Each does not disprove the other. We live in the constant tension of chaos and wonder. My grandfather had the experience and photograph to prove it.

He also taught me that if god really exists, he will prove himself. It wasn't the responsibility of humanity to keep god alive in the collective psyche of the world. If god needed to be propped up by human arguments and straining, what kind of god would he be? My grandpa made it clear that god can take care of himself and would take charge of any need to prove he is around. Watch, my grandfather said. Just keep looking. In no time, you'll see the supernatural. You'll see the unexplainable. You'll see a miracle. In fact, my grandfather emphasized, god will pursue you. Whether I care about god or not, he will chase down whomever he wants. He's the one in charge. He always takes the first step.

That counsel sprang from my grandfather's miraculous experience during World War I. Over nearly a century of life, those principles held true. The contrast of the devastation of war and the delight of an unexpected miracle played out in all of his life experiences. Unlike the philosophers who mused about the existence of god, my grandfather lived in the tense tug of war between utter meaninglessness and the utter miraculous.

He was convinced that science, empirical observation and experimentation, didn't prove the absence of the supernatural, but proved the complexity of the world. The search for knowledge confirmed the presence of what seemed to be endless layers of new discoveries.

He also was certain that the chaos and pain in his life proved the deep and abiding need we have in a turbulent world. In fact, the prevalent hurt and confusion didn't show an absence of the divine, it seemed instead to highlight the appearance of the miraculous.

My grandfather was all about proving what really existed, not what might or might not be absent. He was not

Chapter Ten

someone who would live in denial. He faced the truth of a brutal life with courage and boldness. He also confronted the miraculous, the supernatural, with confidence. He dared to walk in both worlds, seeing how they would play out, not pretending to be bigger than the forces that swelled and raged around him.

I wondered if I could do the same. Could I face reality--all of it? Would I become numbed and apathetic in my thinking, or would I still face the big questions life brought? Could I make it through profound grief without sliding into a temper tantrum of denial or a deluded life of fantasy? Only reality, only indisputable proof, could keep me balanced and guide me through. I needed to face the facts--all of the facts.

I took my wallet out, reached into it, and slowly pulled out a picture. It wasn't my Grandpa Newman's miracle picture. That had disappeared long ago. No, this one was mine. You see, after my Grandpa Hides died, I got a picture of my own miracle.

But that's a story for another time.

Chapter Ten Discussion Questions:
Testing

1. How has this "Tale of Two Grandfathers" affected your life perspective?

2. Sometimes people are made to feel guilty or indecisive if they have doubts. Discuss how doubt is a normal part of human experience.

3. What big questions has this book caused you to think about?

4. In what ways has this book challenged you to live and think differently?

5. What would it take for god to really prove his existence to you?

6. Discuss any other insights, thoughts, or questions this book caused you to think about.

About the Author

Michael Newman remembers his grandfathers fondly and continues to try to ask big questions while watching for the miraculous. Much of his pondering takes place as he logs miles running on the Texas roads. After he earned his degree in philosophy, he went on to complete graduate work in theology. Married to his wife Cindy since 1983, they have been blessed with two wonderful daughters.

For information and to purchase books, go to
www.mnewman.org.

Books are also available at Amazon.com or through your local Barnes and Noble bookseller.

Made in the USA
Charleston, SC
28 September 2012